RIGHT ANGLES

PAPER-FOLDING GEOMETRY

RIGHT ANGLES

PAPER-FOLDING GEOMETRY

By
Jo Phillips

Illustrated by
Giulio Maestro

Thomas Y. Crowell Company / New York

YOUNG MATH BOOKS

Edited by Dr. Max Beberman, Director of the Committee on School Mathematics Projects, University of Illinois

BIGGER AND SMALLER
by Robert Froman

CIRCLES
by Mindel and Harry Sitomer

COMPUTERS
by Jane Jonas Srivastava

THE ELLIPSE
by Mannis Charosh

ESTIMATION
by Charles F. Linn

FRACTIONS ARE PARTS OF THINGS
by J. Richard Dennis

GRAPH GAMES
by Frédérique and Papy

LONG, SHORT, HIGH, LOW, THIN, WIDE
by James T. Fey

ODDS AND EVENS
by Thomas C. O'Brien

PROBABILITY
by Charles F. Linn

RIGHT ANGLES:
PAPER-FOLDING GEOMETRY
by Jo Phillips

RUBBER BANDS, BASEBALLS, AND DOUGHNUTS:
A BOOK ABOUT TOPOLOGY
by Robert Froman

STRAIGHT LINES, PARALLEL LINES
PERPENDICULAR LINES
by Mannis Charosh

WEIGHING & BALANCING
by Jane Jonas Srivastava

WHAT IS SYMMETRY?
by Mindel and Harry Sitomer

Copyright © 1972 by Jo Phillips.
Illustrations copyright © 1972 by Giulio Maestro

All rights reserved. Except for use in a review, the reproduction or utilization of this work in any form or by any electronic, mechanical, or other means, now known or hereafter invented, including xerography, photocopying, and recording, and in any information storage and retrieval system is forbidden without the written permission of the publisher. Published simultaneously in Canada by Fitzhenry & Whiteside Limited, Toronto. Manufactured in the United States of America.

L.C. Card 72-171007
ISBN 0-690-60916-7
0-690-60917-5 (LB)

1 2 3 4 5 6 7 8 9 10

RIGHT ANGLES
PAPER-FOLDING GEOMETRY

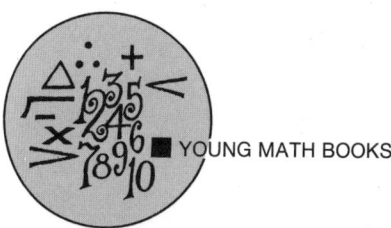
YOUNG MATH BOOKS

To have fun with this book you will need quite a lot of paper.

Sometimes just any paper will do, even newspaper if it is not wrinkled.

Sometimes you need nice clean paper. It should not be very thick. Thin paper is easier to fold. Also, it will be better if your clean paper does not have lines.

You will need scissors, too, and a pencil.

Take a piece of paper. It does not matter whether its edges are straight.

Fold it once, any old way.

Fold it again, but this time line it up so that your first fold falls along itself.

See what you get.

It is a perfect square corner.

A RIGHT ANGLE is another name for square corner. You have a model of a right angle.

The point at the very tip of the corner is the VERTEX of the angle.

Use your right angle to test things in your room. Does the edge of the door make a right angle with the floor? Test by putting the vertex of your right angle on the vertex of the angle you are testing and see whether you can make the sides match.

Does a leg of your chair make a right angle with the floor? (A front leg might; a back leg probably does not.)

If a corner of any object will fit inside your right angle, its edges make an angle smaller than a right angle.

If a corner just lines up with your right angle, it is a square corner. It is a right angle.

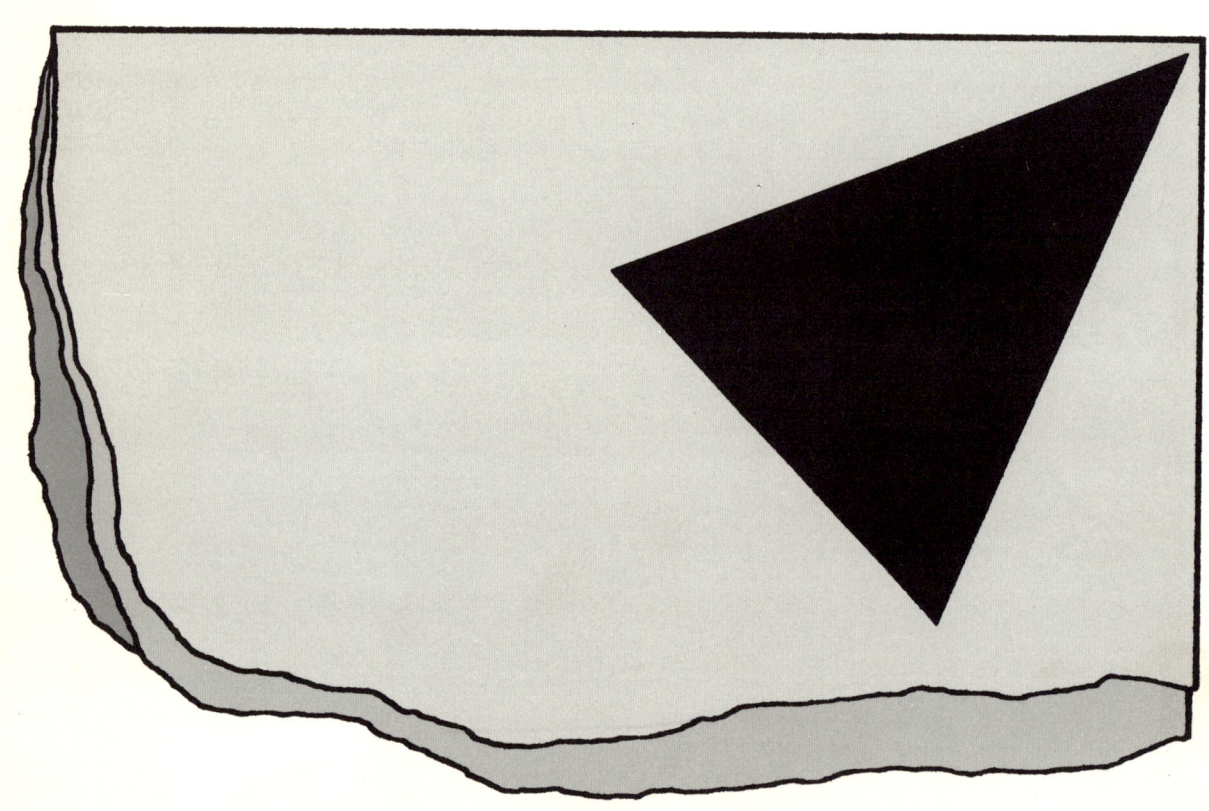

If your right angle fits inside another angle with some space to spare, that angle is bigger than a right angle.

Big angles "have their mouths open wider" than small angles.

See how many right angles you can find in your room. See how many angles smaller than a right angle you can find. See how many angles bigger than a right angle you can find.

Most doors have the shape of a RECTANGLE. So does a side of a box. So does a sheet of typing paper.

You can fold a rectangle, even with paper that has ragged edges.

Take a piece of paper. Fold a right angle somewhere near one edge of your paper.

Fold another right angle. Use one of the folds you made the first time.

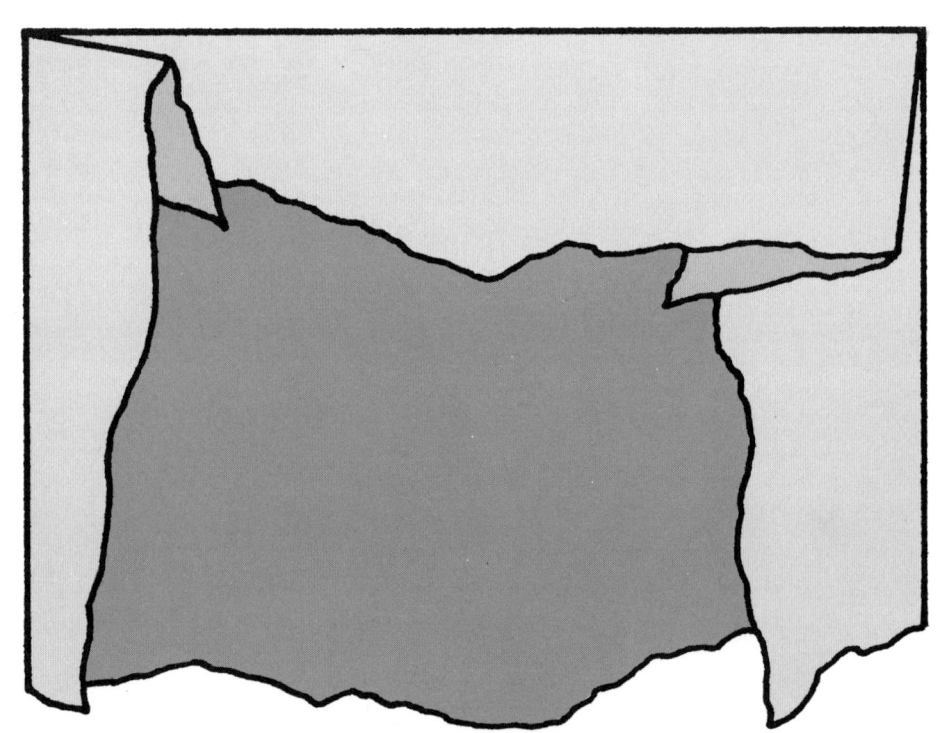

Fold a third right angle. Use one fold you have made before. Do not put a new fold between two you already have.

Did you get a fourth right angle without doing any more folding?

If you did, you have folded a rectangle. A rectangle comes with four right angles. In fact, "rectangle" sounds a little like "right angle."

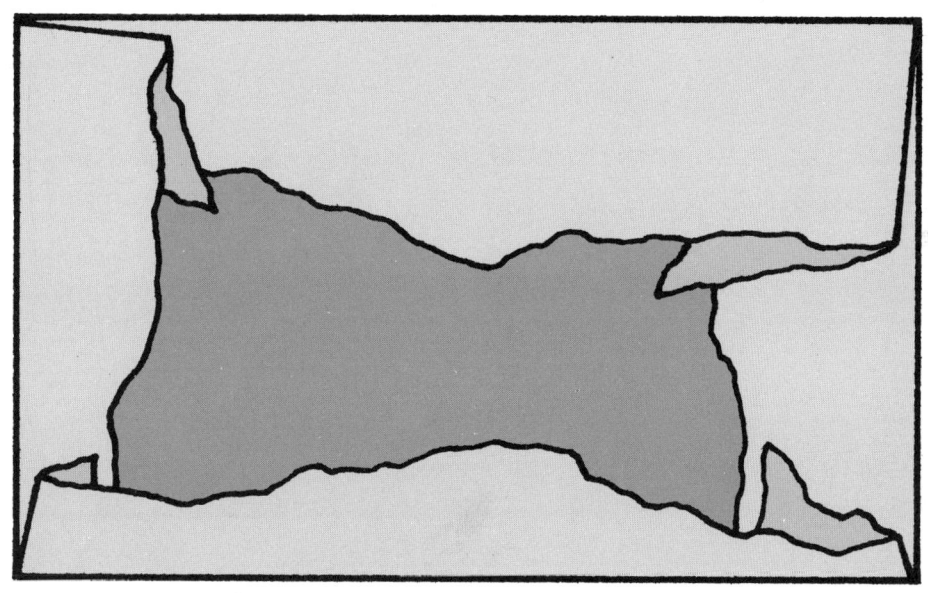

Find some things shaped like rectangles.

You need at least six rectangles now. Either get some pieces of paper shaped like rectangles or fold some rectangles and cut them out. Be sure to fold and cut very carefully.

The edges straight across from each other are OPPOSITE SIDES of a rectangle. Take one of your rectangles. Can you fold it so that one pair of opposite sides just match? If you can, those opposite sides are CONGRUENT. Test the other pair of opposite sides. Are both pairs of opposite sides of a rectangle congruent?

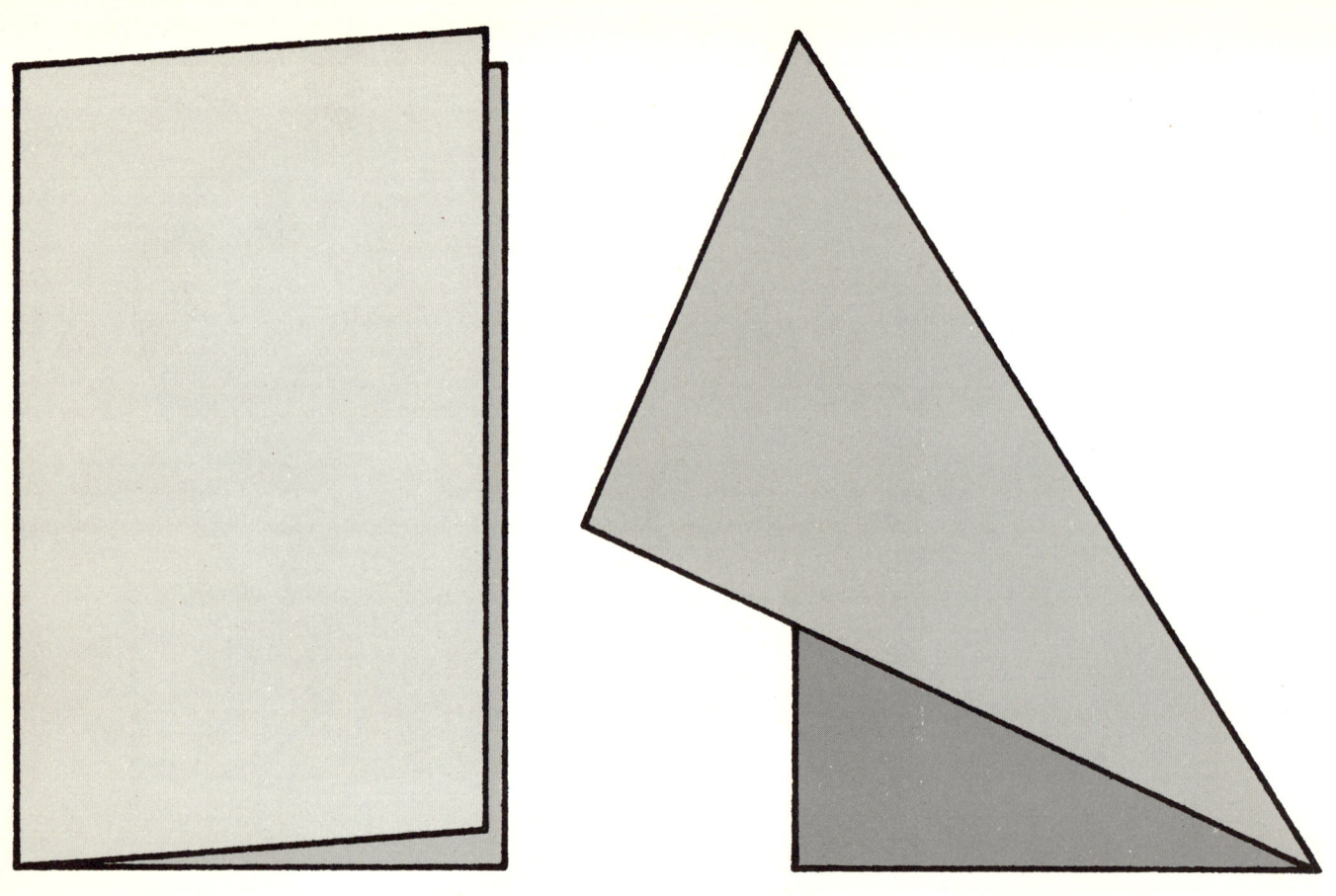

Pretend that each rectangle is a sandwich. See how many ways you can make just one fold so that each of two people can have the same amount to eat. (Use a different piece of paper for each way.)

Test by cutting along the fold and seeing whether the two pieces match. Turn one piece over face down, if you need to. You should find at least four ways to fold a rectangle into congruent halves (congruent because you can make them match, and halves because they are two same-size parts of a whole).

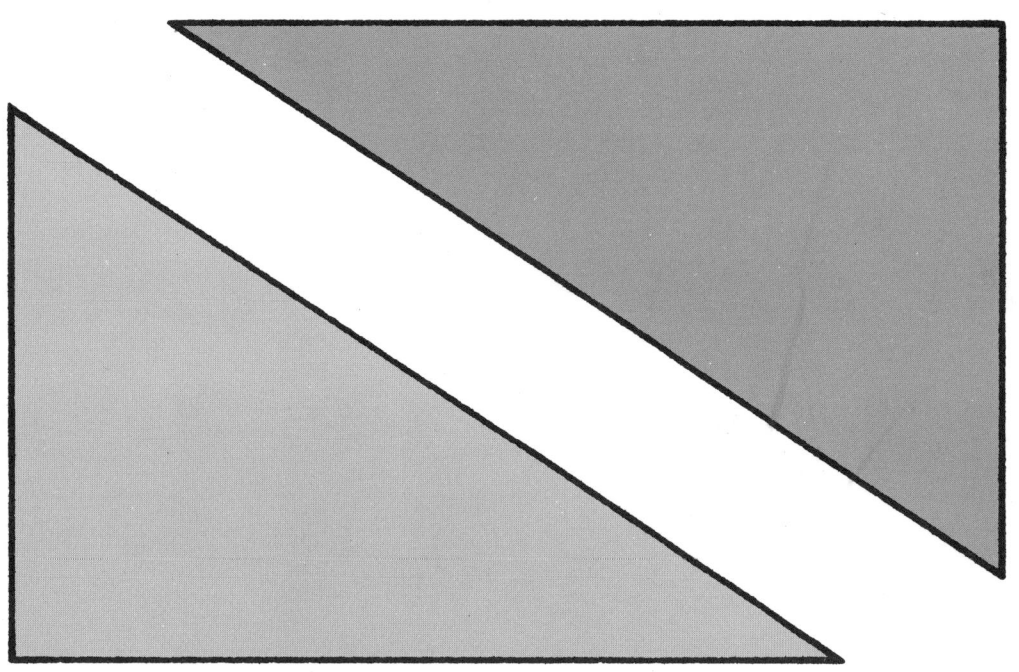

Figure out a way to find the point exactly in the center of a rectangle. Mark that point by making a very small, dark dot with your pencil. Fold the rectangle just any way so that the fold goes through the dot. Cut along the fold. Can you make the pieces match? Now you should be able to find many more ways to fold a rectangular shape into congruent halves.

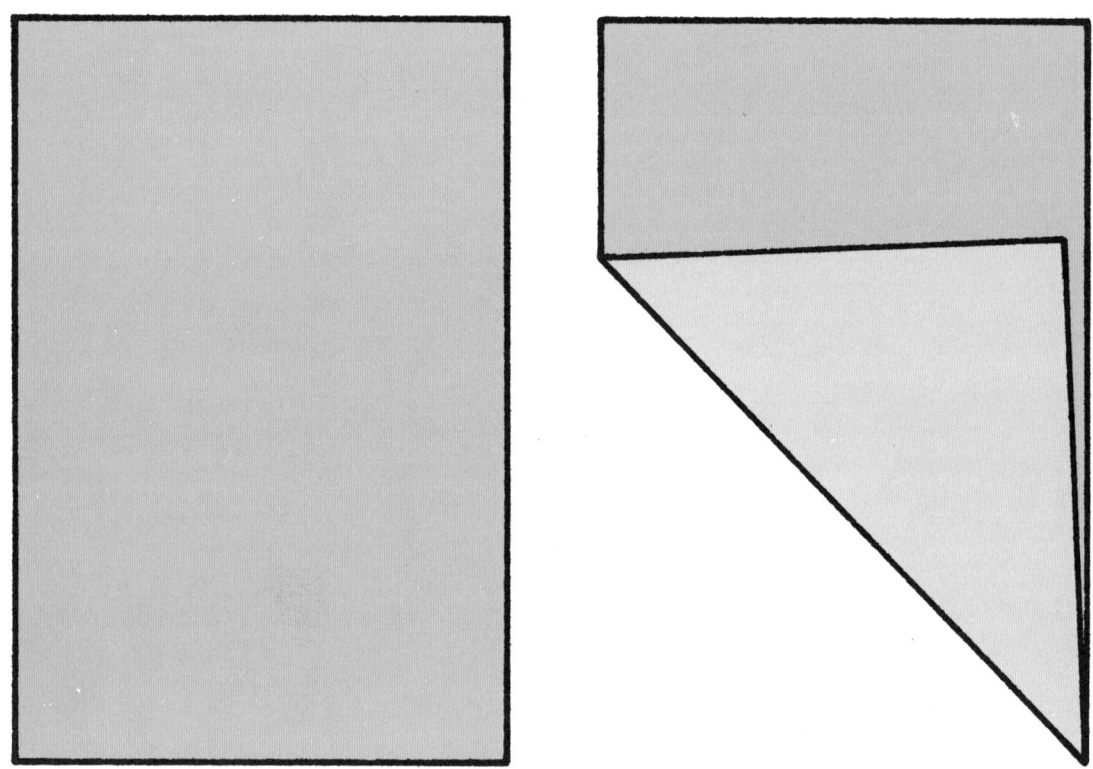

When all four sides of a rectangle are the same length, there is a special name for it. It is a SQUARE. A square is a rectangle with four congruent sides.

You can fold a square.

An easy way to fold a square is to start with a piece of paper shaped like a rectangle. Fold a bottom corner up so that a short side lines up with a long side.

Crease the fold. Now, fold back the flap, the part that is just one layer of paper. Open up the first fold you made. Test the shape you see. Are there four right angles? Are there four congruent sides? If so, it's a square.

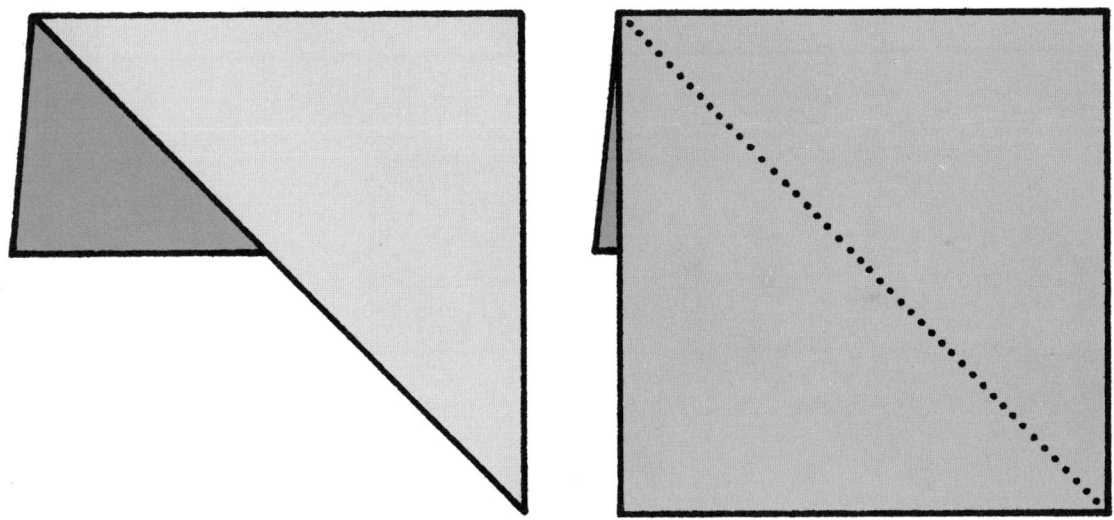

If you want a square that does not have a crease inside it, get your pencil ready. Fold up one corner, as before, very carefully, but do not crease the fold. Mark with your pencil the place where the corner you folded up touches the other side. Do the same thing with the other bottom corner. Then fold your paper through those two marks.

Think of all the things you know about a rectangle. Those same things are all true of a square, too, because squares are special kinds of rectangles. There is at least one more thing true of squares that is not true of rectangles.

Find some things shaped like squares. Notice that all squares look alike, except for size. All squares are SIMILAR.

Not all rectangles are similar. Fold a tall thin rectangle. Fold a rectangle about half as tall as it is wide. Fold a rectangle that is a square. There are many rectangles with shapes that do not look alike.

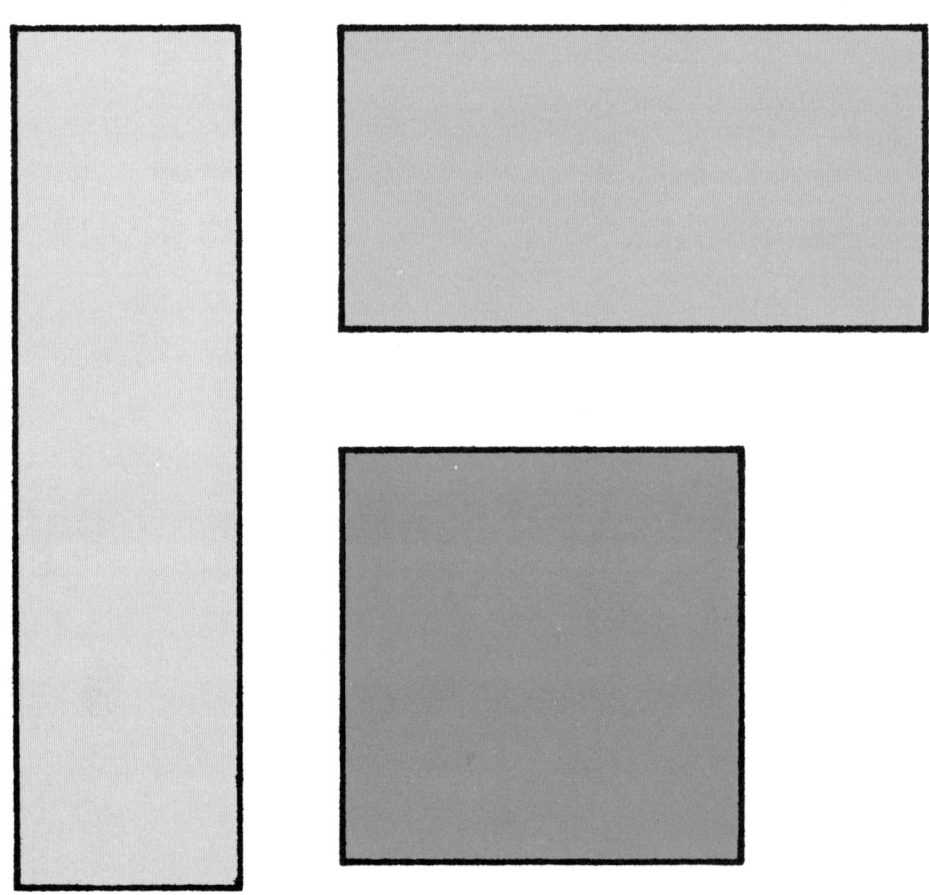

You can make them larger or smaller but they still do not look alike.

A line figure with four straight sides is a QUADRILATERAL. Here are pictures of some shapes a quadrilateral may have.

See whether you can fold a quadrilateral that has no right angles.

Can you fold a quadrilateral that has exactly one right angle? Exactly two right angles? Three right angles? Four? One of those is impossible. You can tell why.

Find some right angles in this picture.

Find some angles bigger than right angles.

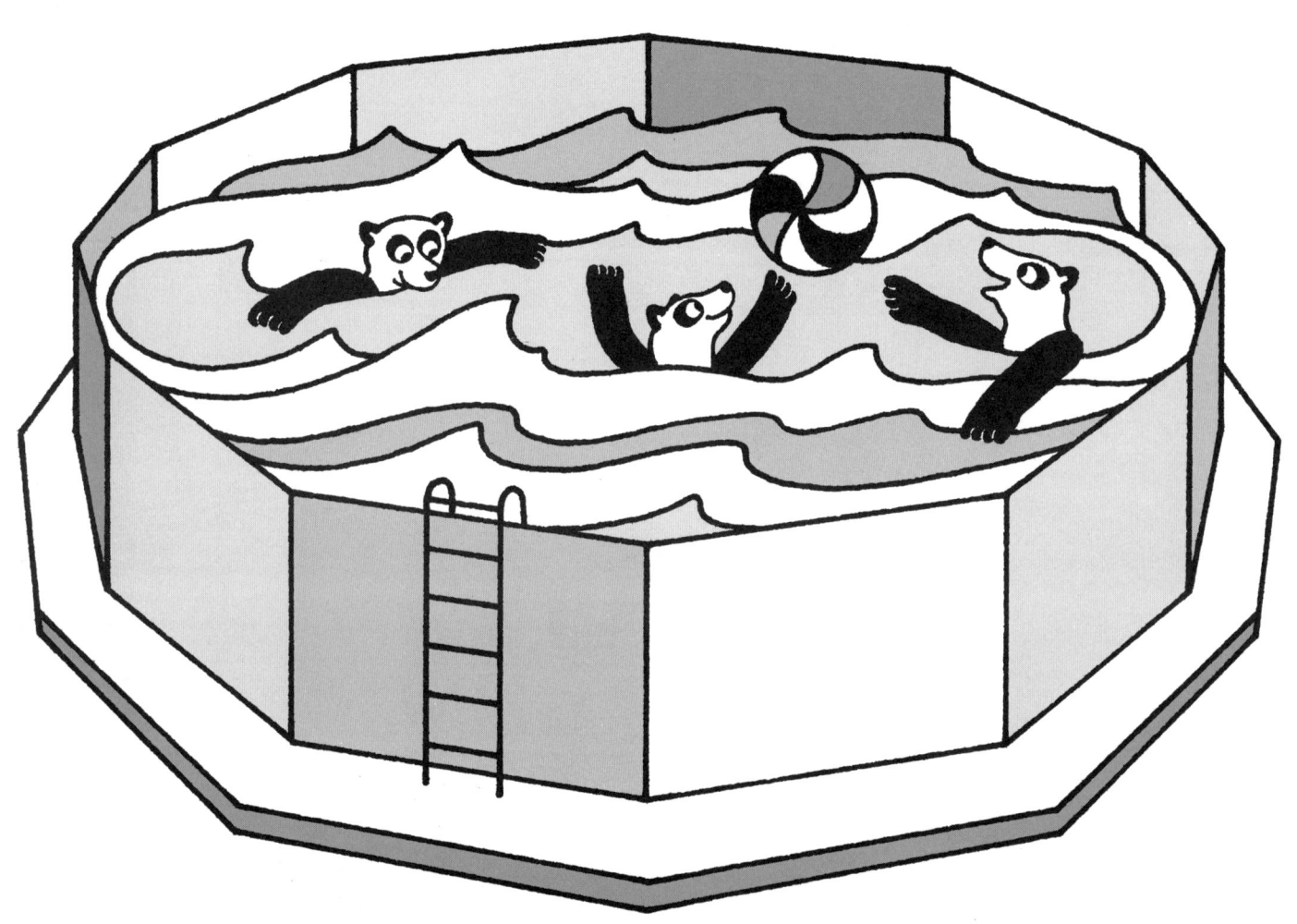

Find some rectangles.

Find some quadrilaterals that are not rectangles. Have fun.

ABOUT THE AUTHOR

Jo Phillips believes that the best way to learn about math is to do projects and experiments. That is one reason why she enjoyed writing RIGHT ANGLES: PAPER-FOLDING GEOMETRY.

Dr. Phillips has taught school at every level from second grade through graduate school; she has also been a textbook editor and an officer in the U.S. Coast Guard. She is now Contributing Editor in Mathematics for *The Instructor* magazine, and teaches teachers of mathematics at the University of Cincinnati.

ABOUT THE ILLUSTRATOR

Giulio Maestro was born in New York City and studied at the Cooper Union Art School and Pratt Graphics Center. Aside from picture-book illustration, he is well-known for his beautiful hand-lettering and book-jacket design. He enjoys etching and painting in his free time.

Giulio Maestro lives with two cats Popi and Thai-Thai who, Mr. Maestro tells us, "provide inspiration for the antics of the animals in my picture books. So I must confess there is a cat hidden inside every panda in this book."